Devotion

Love and the Power of Small Steps

Kim Nicol

ISBN-13: 978-1537175386
ISBN-10: 1537175386

Also by the author:

Offering:
The Gentle Power of Mindfulness to Awaken the Love,
Calm, and Wonder in Everyday Life

For Jessica, who asked
the right question at the right time.

"Attention is the beginning of devotion."

Mary Oliver

Contents

How to Read This Book

You may approach the words gathered here in a few different ways.

You can read the book straight through, from the beginning to the end.

You can open the book at any point and read what is there, and then put it away for a while.

You can ask, "What do I need to know now?" and then open the book, and see what answer you receive.

You can read it all in one go, or slowly, one sip at a time.

Know that as you read the words, you awaken and bring life to them. Anything you find of value, any insight or wisdom, is something which you already possess. The words may help you to access or remember something that is already yours.

No matter how you navigate the words, bring your curiosity, and willingness, and friendship.

You may meet yourself along the way.

Meet each part of yourself with curiosity, willingness, and friendship.

That is how to read this book.

Introduction

My first book, *Offering*, invited you to meet life in a mindful way. With this collection, *Devotion*, I want to show you something about love and the willingness to take small steps, again and again.

When you choose to notice Love in the world, that is also an act of Devotion.

Devotion carries a quality of steadfast commitment, one that is infused with Love. Whereas Duty or Responsibility reside in the head, Devotion sits squarely and securely in the heart. It draws so much power from Love.

There are so many other places you could have chosen to be right now, and yet here you are, somehow, having found these words. As you read them, we create a quiet place in the midst of a very noisy world.

I'm glad you're here.

Ok? Then let's begin.

Part 1:

I will never abandon you.

0.

Come here, my love, and let me have you. I know sometimes you feel lost or scattered. The world is a brilliant place, sometimes noisy, and in the course of exploring you may feel disoriented or alone.

I want to tell you that I am always here for you, my love, devoted to your care and well-being, celebrating your victories and holding you in your grief and pain. Always.

I will never abandon you. Such is Devotion.

1.

Sometimes it's hard to see what the work adds up to. It's hard to know if it's "adding value" or if it's any good.

Sometimes it's enough to wash one dish, do one load of laundry, because that is something that makes a clear difference even in a small way.

Sometimes the only way forward is with very small steps. Your movement might even be mistaken for stillness by those at a distance, or to those obsessed with speed.

Trust in the power and sacred sweetness of that which is small. One breath. One heartbeat. One dish.

Devotion is in these small acts, these gentle ways of being. It is in the moments when you are willing to see some small beauty, to feel some pleasure and delight – no matter what else is happening.

Devotion is not the same as ecstasy, though they can be together at times.

Devotion can be muscle ache and sweat as you climb. It can be dirt under the fingernails, or a short bit of writing that no one reads or comments upon. You don't always see the magic you work in the world.

Sometimes you must choose Devotion to the work, even when you cannot see the effect or result of it.

Sometimes it happens in the dark for a good, long while. Sometimes it happens outside of your view.

"Results" have their own timing.

That's not the part you're in charge of, anyway.

The part you're in charge of is the part right here.

Devotion.

One step. One breath. One heartbeat.

Devotion is *Yes*, it is *Again, my love.*

It is a choice.

It is willingness to love, and to delight. Even in the unknowing and unseeing.

It is willingness to fall in love with the work, and yourself, and the way that you both give birth to each other, when you're willing to be devoted in this small, persistent way.

Devotion is love-driven, and when you have become distracted, or feel overcome by fear or shame or challenge, it is a force which gathers and carries you.

2.

This morning I went to a cafe in a different neighborhood – an effort to try new things, and shift my routines a bit. And while I was there, two friends whom I haven't seen in a while walked in!

After hugs, they said:

"We didn't want to disturb you, because you looked so focused in your writing."

Friends, if you find me out and about the city, you can always come up for Hellos and Hugs!

And also: I'm taking this as an encouraging sign to explore a bit more, and allow for Serendipity to find me.

3.

Remember, my love, that you needn't try so hard all the time. Allow for Serendipity to find you. Be willing to recognize and enjoy it.

4.

And can you fall in love with your own tender heart?

Sometimes the heart breaks open and reveals this wet, ugly, staggering creature. But a bit of warmth, a little space, and it fluffs right up and declares itself with its tiny voice, and begins to explore a world that is made new again.

5.

My love, stay with the part of yourself which you call ugly and weak. Give it space, and time, and love. Allow for what you call "breaking" and remember that you are never broken. You are always whole. Offer yourself tenderness and care.

6.

I was talking with my mom about someone I had dated years ago, whom I recently ran into.

She said, "How is he?"

I said, "Exactly the same! I've changed and grown so much in the last few years. He's stuck in exactly the same place."

She said, "Oh, the poor child. Don't be hard on him. You know, he never had the chance to fail without being watched and criticized. He never learned that it was ok to fail, and move on. So he's very afraid to try things, because of this. Be easy on him."

And she said, "When I was growing up, I didn't get things right all the time. I failed at things. But my parents were so supportive, so encouraging. They never doubted me. I gained confidence. It made me strong. He didn't have that."

And it made me chill out, and see him differently.

Why he's stuck.

Why he's paralyzed with worry.

Why he gets an idea and then attacks his own idea with sharp knives – trying to find all the faults himself, before someone he loves does it to him.

We can carry pain and worry a long time.

I realized I'd been carrying some things, too – judgment, for one – and I didn't need it anymore.

I realized that I could hold compassion and kindness instead.

7.

"You are at exactly the right place, at exactly the right time."

My friend said this to me this morning. I really needed to hear it. Maybe you do, too? So I put it here, just in case.

I love you.

8.

One afternoon I was walking in Beverly Hills and this attractive man said to me, "Beautiful dress. Are you in the fashion industry?"

And I said no, and I smiled, and soon we were talking about meditation and life and creativity, and he invited me to join him for coffee, and I did, and it was all such a lovely and unexpected end to my afternoon!

Sometimes, if you let it, life will surprise you with the most wonderful adventures and kindness.

9.

Toes in the sand, wind in my hair, incoming tide reaches up to my knee.

Evening at hand, I have not a care if the hem of my dress is now wet with the sea.

10.

Good morning, beautiful!

I love the way you bloom.

11.

This happened once.

I ordered toast and Nutella.
My friend ordered granola bowl with yogurt and fruit.

Me: Can I have one of your banana slices?

He: Yes, of course.

. . . I smile and take a banana slice and eat it. . .
. . . I leave to put cream in my coffee. . .
. . . I return to find 2 banana slices on my Nutella toast. . .

Me: You put banana on my Nutella toast?

He: Yeah. I thought you'd like it.

Me: . . .

Sometimes you feel the biggest love in the smallest gestures.

12.

And let this self-awareness invite you to greater intimacy, compassion, and friendship with yourself. . . and so, too, with all beings.

Awareness of one's own fears, insecurities, tenderness, passions, joys, pettiness – all the ways that one is human, and fully human – let that be a light by which we recognize one another.

Self-awareness is not for pride or distancing oneself – "Look how evolved I am! Go me! Good job!"

It is for intimacy. It is for kindness. It is for deep connection and appreciation.

It allows us to be truly present with the complexity and chaos and variability of what it is to be human.

So that we can be willing to bring full and unconditional loving kindness to ourselves – and then, to others.

This is a way to live fully.

13.

You were beautiful before you knew the word, and before anyone ever said to you, *You are beautiful.*

You were loved before you knew the word, and before anyone ever said to you, *I love you.*

Your contributions mattered before you knew exactly what they were, or what they would add up to, and before anyone else could see them or recognize them.

Do you hear me, my love? You are beautiful and loved and you matter. Right now. Just as you are. This has always been true, since the beginning.

It is good to remember this.

When you go to the place of forgetting, you will look to others outside you to tell you that you are beautiful, that you are loved, and that your contributions matter. You will spend a lot of time and energy trying to get something that was always yours, that can neither be lost nor earned.

And there is other work for you to do.

So let me whisper it again, quietly, my love, so that you remember this for yourself.

You are beautiful, and you are loved, and you matter, my love. This was true before you knew the words, and before anyone spoke them to you.

14.

Good morning, you beautiful creature!

Today's interior conversation begins like this:

What do you want to be when you grow up?

I want to be prolific.

I want to create a lot, to gather and shape and arrange and design and release. . .

I want to leave a body of work that continues my contribution and usefulness and loving momentum.

It feels so good to give like that.

15.

Your body is amazing.

The body you have today is not the body you were born with.

The body you were born with was much. . . smaller.

You've grown, see?

And every day your body is a little bit different.

That's why it is so important to remember and celebrate and love and cherish the body you have *right now*. Because it is going to change.

The body you have Right Now has been through a lot.

Can you be willing to love it? And enjoy how it feels to move and rest and nourish your sweet body?

Can you feel how delicious it feels to just breathe?

To feel your heart beat?

When you shower, can you feel how good it feels to feel the water running over your skin, from head to toe?

Can you love every part?

From your baby toe, to your belly button, to the sweet bend in your elbow, to your perfectly shaped earlobe?

Can you enjoy how it feels to have a body, even if it's different from how it used to be or from how you want it to be?

Could we try this? The love and enjoyment part of having a body?

16.

Be the _____* you want to see in the world.

*love
*peace
*friendship
*kindness
*goofy joke
*picnic
*nap
*creative play

*love story

*beauty

*courage

*forgiveness

*delight

*sharing food with loved ones

*making new friends

*road trip

*service

*leadership

*mind-bendingly satisfying and healthy sexuality

*patience

*communication

*freedom

*pleasure

*puzzle-solver

*positive, radiant force of nature

*_____ (what else? tell me. in a comment)

PS - YOU ARE ALL THESE THINGS

I love you.

17.

There are many ways to be creative, and so many reasons why.

Today, I'm listening very closely to what is wanting to come forth through me.

And I'm remembering how creation can come, first, by creating a Right Environment – safety, nourishment, rest.

Remembering that Gestation demands Right Environment, and that onlookers cannot see the power and creative forces at play beneath the surface.

Which is why it is so important to remain devoted to what Gestation needs, even when others are casting doubtful glances, wondering where your Productivity is.

(Especially if it's from within.)

It is no surprise that Self-Doubt comes so quickly, for you have lived in an environment that doubts so quickly and so willingly.

Today I practice: Self-Care, Self-Trust, and Self-Respect. I practice Listening, and Allowing Desire.

And I am remembering, also, that to those who move at a frenzied pace, the rest of the world becomes a blur and disappears before their very eyes. The loudness obliterates every other gentler sound. And so it is so easy to become unseen and unheard to those who become addicted to speed and velocity, who become forgetful when living in that state of self-induced blindness and deafness.

I get it. I've been on both sides.

Right now I'm on this side. On my side. On the side of Creation, and Gestation, and all the wisdom and power that moves in the Deep Inside.

18.

Someone said to me, "Do you know _____ ? It's a healing practice, it helps me sleep. It's not backed by science or anything. It sounds a little crazy now that I'm talking about it."

And I said, "Well, remember that science is a way of seeing – that the thing exists before science recognizes it. And if this practice that you love, and that works for you, isn't backed by science maybe it's because science hasn't looked at it yet."

And they said, "I hadn't thought of it that way. Thank you."

And they seemed more relaxed and happy. Less apologetic and shame-tinted.

I have a friend who once said, "I hate this woo-woo stuff! I'm a scientist, and a tech geek. But! I also like to believe in fairies."

And I LOVE THAT.

Because you're big like that.

This is not a new idea.

Remember that Walt Whitman poem:

Do I contradict myself?
Then I contradict myself.
I am vast. I contain multitudes.

Yes, my love, like that.

Science and Woo are not mutually exclusive. There's a lot of science that's pretty woo-woo, when you get down to it. And a lot of woo that, turns out, science says Yes to.

Head and Heart don't need to fight one another.

They are different ways of seeing and knowing.

They work best when they are in friendship with each other.

When opposed, it's just another war.

You are vast. You contain multitudes.

19.

I was talking with someone about meditation, and I said, "For some people, sitting meditation isn't that great for them. A walking meditation can be better. Do you know Grace Cathedral, up on Nob Hill? They have two labyrinths, one inside and one outside. They're the best! I love them for a walking meditation."

He didn't know about the labyrinths. Or about walking meditation. So I thought I'd mention both here, in case that's true for you, too.

I like the labyrinth because it gives my body a way to participate – and at the same time my brain doesn't have to make any decisions, it just pays some light attention to the path, and taking one step at a time.

The switchbacks and turns feel good, too, like being danced.

I find a rhythm of step, breath, heart, and it's very easeful for my mind. The movement helps me to be here, in the present moment, and it helps me to become more receptive.

It's quite a lovely thing.

20.

Sometimes people introduce me as a "meditation guru" – kind of like how you'd call someone a ninja who isn't, you know, an *actual* ninja?

And I say: "Actually, no, I'm not a guru. I'm more like a doorman."

As in, I'll open a door and say, Come on in!

And you know, there are a lot of doors. I don't have the only door, there are doors all over the place. I just happen to be by *this* door, so I'll open it and invite you in. And then you can explore, find your people, find your teachers, find what brings you back home to you.

That's how I feel about it, anyway.

21.

I've been reading and following Byron Katie for a while, and today I'm thinking of some of her words – "Don't argue with reality." I'm noticing how much of the pain we create – or, to bring it down to a very personal level – the pain that *I* create – lives in the world of "should" – an invented gap between what is and what *should* be.

It can sound like this:

"I should be cooking more."
"I should be further along."
"I should have figured this out by now."
"This part of my body should be bigger / smaller."
"My career or business should look different than it looks."
"They shouldn't be like that."
"You shouldn't say that."
"That shouldn't happen."
"Should I be married by now?"
"Should I _____ more / less?"

Arguing with reality. It can be very exhausting, and create a lot of anxiety and insecurity and sometimes anger.

There's an imaginary version of the world, and then there's what's happening now, and the gap is the Should and that's where the pain is.

We do this all the time.

I do this, too.

I suppose it's a human thing.

Humans can get very defensive about their Shoulds. Very justified in having them.

A while back I was talking with an investor who also meditates. He sits on a few boards and has been advising entrepreneurs for years. He says, "It's a competitive advantage to see reality as it is."

I'm thinking about that, too. It's another way of saying, "Don't argue with reality" and "Mind the gap" and "Don't Should yourself."

I'm trying to notice the subtle Shoulds, and instead ask questions like:

What's True?
What else is True?
What do you Desire?
What are you Curious about?
Where are you Willing?
Shall we just go for a walk?

22.

Shame is so interesting, the way it can appear out of nowhere.

About a month ago I was Skyping with a friend in another timezone, and they were telling me about what they'd made for dinner.

And I felt this scared feeling, and it must have shown on my face, because they asked if I was ok.

And I said:

"I. . . I don't think I do that."

"Do what?"

"Make dinner."

"What do you mean?"

"I mean, I eat food at night. Last night I ate. . . beef jerky. And a yogurt. And ice-cream. And, like, three pieces of toast."

"That's ok. We all do that sometimes."

"But I don't eat *meals*. I don't do real dinner! I Very Hungry Caterpillar my way through my kitchen until I'm done."

And I have to tell you, I felt so exposed and ashamed, like I was failing at Something Important.

And I'm remembering this right now because I was just at the grocery store feeling overwhelmed.

What to do with all this? I know people buy food and put it together to make something called "meals" – and I know how to do scrambles, and lentil soup, and I used to know a really good pasta sauce but now I feel really out of my depth here, and the truth is I was feeling ashamed about it.

And I took a deep breath, and since I've been writing about Desire I thought: Well, what I really Desire is to get better at this.

So I emailed my friend and asked if they would help me get better with groceries and cooking and food.

It felt like a courageous ask.

Eating is something I mostly do alone, you know. Most people don't know about how I relate to food.

(If you read my first book, you know about my thing with salad.)

So I'm feeling a little better, now that I've reached out to my friend for help and am revealing this here for you to see.

And if you're feeling shame around something – especially if it's the kind of thing you're afraid others will laugh at, because it seems so ridiculous – it's ok. I understand, believe me.

And what helps, sometimes, is finding the Desire – where you'd like to be. And let that Desire pull you out of the Shame Pit and towards that new place – it can be very clarifying, and help focus on what matters.

Desire can hold your hand and help guide you out of the dark.

23.

There is Cancer in my family. It lives and has lived in the bodies of those I love.

And so, in a way, I love Cancer.

Because I am unwilling to reject or hate any part of those I love.

I choose to love entirely – the cells we call Healthy, and the forgetful ones we call Cancer.

I am so grateful just to be here. To know you, and love you, and be on the planet with you.

I love every cell of your body and being, without reserve.

Try it. Love every cell of your body, without reserve. It might be hard at first. It might take some practice. See what happens.

You're worth it.

24.

Empathy is about feels, not circumstances – so it's not "how would I feel if I was in the circumstance you're in" because that's an opinion about the circumstances, plus a judgement or evaluation of the subsequent feels.

Rather – it's recognizing the emotion the other person has and knowing from the inside of yourself what that emotion feels like.

That's why it is so important to be aware of and in peaceful relationship with your range of emotion – to allow yourself to feel your feels. To get familiar with them, so you can recognize them.

This doesn't mean letting them drive the bus. Can you feel them, without letting them drive the bus?

It takes a bit of practice.

It can be intense. Kinda scary at times.

It's a very intimate practice. First, being willing to connect with your own emotional range. And then, being willing to connect with another human from that place.

Not always easy, making those connections and moving through life as a feeling creature.

I wouldn't trade it, though.

It's what makes it possible for me to love you this much.

25.

Today I was on my way to an event downtown, and I walked by this big construction site – lots of activity – and there was an older guy in an orange vest and hardhat, and also a cop at the intersection – and as I approached the guy in the vest saw me and held out his sign – the one that says STOP on one side and SLOW on the other – and the cop stepped into the road — so that a big truck could exit the site. . .

And so I stopped (like the sign said), and everyone did their part, like this dance with big construction vehicle – like something out of Fantasia – and then we all went back to place and I continued on my journey. . .

And I thought:

"Wow, thank you guys for helping to keep me safe."

And when I thought about it, I realized that there are SO MANY people who work to help keep me safe. The Muni driver, the people who do maintenance on the busses and BART tracks, the construction guy with the sign, the cop helping to direct traffic, the crossing guard in front of the school. . .

So many people show up and do the not-always-visible, easily-taken-for-granted, un-glamorous work of keeping me safe, and all of us safe.

And I felt so cared for, by so many strangers, and I thought that was a beautiful thing.

There are so many people watching out for you. Wanting you to get across the street safely, wanting you to get home or to wherever you're going, safely.

Isn't it nice to know?

26.

Sometimes you make plans, and Love says, "Pssssst, hey, you got a minute?"

And you happily say, "Yes!" and drop your plans so you can turn to Love with open arms and go all in on a big hug.

27.

I was at a party and someone asked me, "What do you do?" And I smiled and said, "Hmm. . . ask me a different question." And they said, "Ok, what lights you up?"

And I said, "Oh, that's a good question! There are lots of things. Just today, I meditated in a police station with two other amazing people. . ."

And then I said, "What about you?"

And we were off and running into a beautiful flow of conversation about things that we were excited about, and working on.

It's a reminder that:

1) The Quality of your Question will inform the Quality of your Connection

and

2) It's ok to Ask for what you want – you can do so in a way that brings more connection, play, energy, and fun into a situation.

28.

You are remarkable. Powerful. Beautiful. Caring. Strong. You judge yourself so harshly, but that's because you have such high expectations for what you should be. The person you want to be isn't half as amazing as the person you already are.

29.

Me: "You're so good to me."

He: "For you. With you."

I did not realize how guarded I had become with my heart, until it broke open and let him in.

30.

Yesterday someone asked me how I had the confidence to try so many things, and go for so many things in my life and career.

But it isn't confidence. It's curiosity. Curiosity and doing things quietly is how it has always worked for me. I don't know how it goes for others. I just know that being curious is the spark, and being quiet is what saves me time – no need to explain or justify to anyone. Just go.

31.

We can get so twisted up about change – wanting it desperately, fearing it deeply, demanding it from others and refusing it when others do the same to us.

And look how the sky and ocean change, how the light and colors and movement shift.

Ever changing. Gentle, yet powerful. Magnificent.

Like you.

32.

Sometimes the best that words can do is suggest the shape or shadow of the essence, make a helpless and ungainly attempt to deliver with any real accuracy or fidelity that which yearns to be conveyed – that which has been touched, held, and seeks to be expressed, shared.

Yet there is, still, Grace in the sweet effort, and the earnest endeavor is not without merit and deserves a kind of honor, or at least a kind nod for the willing hope in hopelessness.

All of which is a long road to saying:

I love you.

And I remain, always, your devoted friend.

Part 2:

Love will always find you.

33.

And I needed to walk, and to think, and feel, and read. And I wanted coffee. And so I walk a mile or so and end up at a cafe I've never been to before. I have coffee and I journal and I read. And I hear a voice call my name and I look up and see a sweet soul, whom I haven't seen in some time. And I smile and stand and we hug, before parting to continue along the path of our day.

Love will always find you. Even if you find yourself somewhere new. Even if you're not looking.

Love will always find you.

34.

Endings, and beginnings. Closing, and opening. Inhale, and exhale.

I love breakfast. But it's a good thing that breakfast ends, so that then I can have lunch.

And I love lunch! But it's a good thing that lunch ends, so that later I can then have dinner.

And I love dinner! But it's a good thing that dinner ends, so that I can have dessert. And then sleep. And then begin a new day.

The ONLY way that it's possible to experience and fully enjoy Breakfast, and Lunch, and Dinner, and Dessert – is by allowing each to end.

It's all like this, friends.

The ending is a beautiful part of the pleasure, the enjoyment, the journey, the discovery, the deepening, the experience of living into Life.

And I'm thinking about this a lot because the startup I've been working with the last 7-ish months has come to a close. It's no longer operating, and the team is now moving on and forward.

Part of it is hard, because there is so much that felt good about working together and it feels like there's so much more to do.

But it also feels good, because we have all gained learnings and relationships in the experience, and many of us will continue to work together – just in a different shape.

What if a job was like an incredible meal. What if a company was like a glorious dinner party. Where people gather to contribute to creating something incredible – and it will come, ultimately, to an end, as we find our fill, or our appetites change, or we move on to explore new cuisine and company.

Show up at the table. Be there fully. Contribute honestly. Receive with pleasure.

And when it's time, forks down and step away from your plate.

Sometimes it's BBQ and you eat with your bare hands and it gets all over everything and it's a delicious mess.

Sometimes it's an exquisite sushi spread and each bite is carefully arranged and you eat with chopsticks, very precise.

Sometimes it makes you cry, it's so intense, and so good. Sometimes it makes you ill, you went overboard or it just didn't agree with you.

Every bite will nourish you because it gives you new learnings, new experiences, new relationships, new perspectives.

Maybe it's like that.

35.

I love onions! And not just the eating of them, which is delicious, but I have fallen in love with the living power of onions.

Or perhaps more accurately: with the way onions teach and remind me of the power of life.

I cut these and sautéed them for an egg scramble.

Then I let them sit on the counter and look!

See how they grow.

See how life keeps reaching through them, how they rise with such devotion and quiet persistence.

See how wakeful and aroused they are – how they move and extend.

Onions say, "I'm here to live. Let's go!"

Teachers are everywhere in your life.

36.

And by "healing," I mean "whole."

As in: feeling fully accepted, and welcomed, and seen, and loved.
As in: allowing space for all of your desires and fears, insecurities and passions.
As in: receiving and replenishing, and reaching and giving.
As in: inhale, and exhale.
As in: sex and career and creativity and friendship.
As in: connection to your deepest self, and wounded self, and brilliant self.

As in: your unique power, and your powerful tenderness.

As in: all the things of being a human.

All The Things.

The Wholeness of it.

37.

I didn't realize what a controlling person I was until I met someone who just showed up in my life and loved me – completely, unexpectedly, and fully.

And I thought, "Wait, but I didn't do anything to try to make you love me. I didn't do my little tricks, I didn't try to make myself into the person I thought you wanted, I didn't try to be who I thought I needed to be in order for you to love me."

And my friend says, "Yeah."

"Wait, so I was just me and you love me?"

"Yep."

I didn't realize how much I'd been trying to control and manipulate others into loving me. (I'm sorry.)

I didn't realize how much I thought that just being myself wasn't enough.

I didn't realize I thought that love was a prize to be rewarded for Doing Things Right and for Being a Certain Way.

I have Powerful Emotions, and Bad Days, and I have sometimes Scared or So Judgmental or Impatient.

And my friend says, "It's ok. You're allowed. And by the way: me, too."

And this person just loves me, Even Though.

It's fascinating to me.

And it makes me think there are other friends in my life who love me the same – but I haven't really given them the chance, because I've been too busy trying to control things.

(I'm sorry.)

I did not expect to learn this about myself in this way.

And so I am also learning also about Forgiveness, and Compassion.

And Surrender, and deep Gratitude.

38.

I love you so much, it hurts.

And by "hurt" I mean achy and tender, like that feeling when you've done a bunch of squats and it's making you so present and so strong, or you've gone hiking and gained some altitude and you feel that deep burn and at the same time you feel light headed and uplifted and like you're going to explode or dissolve because it just feels so damn good to be alive and sweating and breathing and growing and being right here right now, together, looking across the horizon and taking it all in.

That's how I feel about you, and us, right now. On this journey together.

Kind of intense. In the very best way.

39.

Sometimes when I feel myself want something, it's followed by a feeling of shame or discouragement – and other times, it's followed by a feeling of warmth and enthusiasm.

Either way, Desire is a call to pay close attention, and to listen to the Deep Inside with Curiosity, Love, and Kindness.

So hold space for Desire. Allow it to be there, along with all the other feels that follow it into the room. It's all there to help you see yourself better, to create more intimacy and awareness.

And these are magnificent gifts, that you alone have the power to claim.

40.

Did you notice that Spring is here, asserting herself? The sun and the rain, the flowers and growing things – the variability and tenderness – the intense and magnificent and unapologetic way that Life moves.

41.

There was a girl who was drunk, and her heart was breaking, and somehow she fell in love with me, or something that seemed like love, or love enough from where she stood –

. . .and things started to go badly for her, and she was passing out, and her friend managed to get her cell phone and called the girl's husband to come pick her up –

. . .and the bouncer said she had to go, and we said, "Yeah, we're trying," and she was collapsing and what happened was that I managed to get her outside, and waited with her, she was semi-conscious now –

. . .I spoke sweetly to her and petted her hair and held her hand –

. . .and a car pulled up and the friend opened the door and talked briefly with the man, whom I assumed was her husband, and we got her into the passenger seat and put the seatbelt on her, and he drove away –

. . .and I never learned what happened to her, or who she was, or if she became happy again –

. . .but the bouncer and I became friends, kind of, the way you become friends when you've been through something together –

. . .and even though I so very rarely drink I do walk by that bar from time to time –

. . .and whenever he is working the front door I swoop in for a hug –

. . .and he opens his arms to me, and gives the best hugs, and I'm glad that we have each other, in this small way –

. . .that we have this beautiful connection, that arose from a dark and difficult night, of being human together.

42.

Sometimes I'm just walking somewhere and I see someone I know and we hug. That is one of the best things ever.

43.

Tonight was amazing – a wonderful gathering of fabulous people, we talked about All The Things – meditation, mindfulness, risk / change, sex, relationships. . . We talked about Things That Are Great, and also Things That Are Hard. We talked about how to make room for All The Things – to embrace and meet All of Life, mindfully.

So I also want to tell you that earlier today I had a lot of Sadness, and was having a Very Hard Time.

I texted a friend for support.

After a few messages exchanged, this:

He: Have you rediscovered your radiance?

Me: Getting there. I do have a bit more purrrr in me now.

He: Good. A little more purrr is a great thing to have, but don't forget that I love you even if you're purrrrless.

Me: That means so much to me.

He: I wasn't trying to repurrrrr you, by the way. I just wanted to know if you had repurrred yourself.

And then, later in the day:

Me: I'm radiant again!

He: You never stopped, my love.

It feels amazing to allow All The Things. To accept and feel accepted, just as one is in the moment. To have friends who remind you that you are still loved and cared for when you have an off day, or when you're feeling sad or messy.

This is also the gift you have the power to give – not needing others to be happy, accepting and loving them when they're having a hard time, not being pulled into their story but also not trying to solve their problems or find a solution.

Just Be with them and Love them.

It feels so good, and is so healing.

And by Healing I mean Whole. Which is about making room for All The Things, and all the ways we are human.

Grrrs and purrrrs. . .

44.

Sometimes the things we do not plan for — could not possibly plan for — are what change our life in the most profound and delightful way. A chance encounter in an elevator. An unexpected invitation. A conversation with or even just a glance from a kind stranger.

It's good to remember this because sometimes we get so worried about all the doing and the not doing-enoughs. Sometimes just show up and listen. Just show up to what's in front of you. You don't need to be in charge of making it happen.

You just need to Be.

45.

Me: "I feel honored that you'd take the trouble to meet with me."

He: "Honored? I just feel lucky."

Me: *blush*

46.

In my classes I've been having my students draw. Simple things.
A heart. A flower. A cat.

"Why are you here?"

I tell them to write the answer on a card. And then to draw a
heart. A flower. A cat.

The heart is for love. Because we so often withhold it from ourselves.

The flower is for growth, and tenderness. When we learn new
things it can feel vulnerable – we're extending ourselves, like a
tender shoot coming up out of the earth and looking for sun.

The cat is for curiosity, and for play. Curiosity is your ally in all
things. Play is good to bring into the mix.

47.

Love can only heal what presents itself to be loved and healed.

Sometimes when we love, the most tender and terrified parts
begin to surface – the deep wounds rise, they want to be seen at
last, and accepted, and loved, and claimed as a beloved part of
the whole of who you are.

This can feel scary.

Especially if you've become very good, over many years, at being controlled over such things. The resurfacing feels like a loss of control, and an intense vulnerability.

Love stays. Love holds space.

Love says, "Yes, come, I want to see you, I want all of you, I want to witness you at your most desperate and vulnerable. I want to love every part of you. Show me who you are, show me everything. I am here."

And while it's ultimately something we must do for ourselves, it is also true that the loving presence of another can facilitate this.

Sometimes we need a safe place to fall apart, so we can see clearly and reclaim every piece. Especially the bits we've struggled to love, that are perhaps hidden or buried deep in the dark.

48.

I want to remind you that you are a beautiful human, and very much loved. Just in case you forgot.

49.

Me: "One day I want you to come with me to the island."

He: "I'd like that."

Me: "There is a hammock, and two people can fit in it, and at night we could be in the hammock together and look up at the stars. . . There are so many stars! You won't believe how many stars there are."

He: "I like stargazing. It's my second favorite thing to do at night."

Me: *blush*

50.

You're powerful in unexpected ways, he said.

And I smiled, and sighed.

Yes, like that.

51.

And this is a reminder.

That you don't always receive Love in the format you prefer, sometimes it's also cluttered with debris and junky stuff. Or it shows up looking completely different than what you'd been led to believe to expect.

But you know what, it really doesn't matter. Receive Love, Unconditionally. Receive the Love, let go of the rest. That Love is Yours to keep.

Too often we put so many conditions on Love – it has to look exactly like this, or I'm not allowed to receive it until I've accomplished or proven this thing.

That's all crap, darling.

Receive love, unconditionally.

Just try it for a day.

You can always go back to the other way, if you want.

52.

The sunset is breathtaking – an impossible color – there is no name for the colors in the sky.

And it doesn't matter that it's changing and can't be captured or kept.

The moment is mine forever, completely, because I am here –
fully present and open to this.

And it reminds me to Allow Love, fully, without reservation or
demand that it stay or remain unchanging.

If I can be Willing, Glad, Open, and Present to the sky, perhaps
I can meet Love in the same way.

53.

You know, sometimes you don't have to try so hard for life to
be amazing. Most of the time it *wants* to be amazing for you,
but you're so locked into your own schedule that the amazing
stuff can't get in or you speed by it without letting it fully land.

It's good to breathe, to leave space for Serendipity, to be open
and ok with Not Knowing Things.

54.

My Head: "But this is Impractical. Foolhardy. Absurd."

My Intuition: "It seems so because of your current view, which
is limited. There is something of great value here for you. And
while the words you use to describe this may, in a sense, be True,
they are neither All nor Sufficient."

My Heart: "Desire. Courage. I am willing and eager."

My Gut: "Trust me. We're ready for this."

My Head: "Ok then. I'm in."

55.

I'm in New York and thinking about love, and aloneness, and togetherness, and adventure, and creativity.

The part I really want you to know right now is this: I love you. And even the messy parts, the confusing parts, the "not-at-all-together" parts – I love all of it, and all of you.

Because I'm like that, too. I have all those parts.

The more I practice seeing them, and meeting them with tenderness and friendship, the more I can meet others with the same generosity of heart and spirit.

56.

Sometimes the way you make the world a better place is simply by connecting two people who need to know each other.

57.

He: "How are you today?"

Me: "I'm good. No, I'm. . . frustrated. No, I'm . . . angry. I'm angry! I am angry today."

He: "Want to talk about it?"

Me: "No. I don't want to bring that energy into the space. I want to to go for walk and stomp around in the park."

He: "Can I come?"

Me: (big smile, laughter) "Yes! Let's go to the park and have an angry, stompy walk. I'd love that."

Acceptance doesn't mean dwelling or giving up. Allow for what's true to be there. And then choose how you'd like to handle it.

58.

Meet today like a lover: present, ready, willing, devoted, and with much delight for how you will play together, what you will discover, what new angles and cadence you might try.

59.

I wanna just wrestle Life to the ground and lick its face. That's how good and alive I feel right now.

60.

"So tell me about this hot date you have this weekend," he said.

"Well," I said, "She's tall and has this amazing hair. And she's smart, and has a goofy sense of humor – which I love! And she's open and really interesting, and she even wrote a book! I'm super excited to hang out with her. I just know we're going to have an incredible time."

"You're talking about yourself, aren't you?"

"Yes!"

I used to feel such anxiety and insecurity around Valentine's Day and whether I was or was not a part of a couple.

Today I just feel so happy to be alive, enjoying my friendships and connections and flirting with the sky and the trees.

61.

Love on the exhale. Full breath in, and then: love, love, love. . .

62.

It's hard to remember how to go deep when you only measure velocity. When acceleration is your obsession and priority, it's easy to miss depth.

Because to access depth you need presence, stillness, and space away from the noise and distractions you love / hate so much.

Depth is core. Depth is foundation. Depth is deep inner drive and purpose. All the things that pull the strings are rooted deep within – the fears and desires and longings that you've never really taken the time to get to know or put words to.

Assumptions and beliefs live deep, and they like it because it means you almost never pause to get to know or question them.

You might even be afraid of the depths within. You might be afraid of stillness and presence. Consider the efforts you go to avoid them, and all of the reasons.

Your mind has all the reasons why you have no time for depth, for stillness, for rest, for presence.

It isn't true.

The truth is that it's a choice you make

63.

Someone sent me this message:

I am convinced you are an angel in human form, and that the spirits work through you to help me in my own life journey.

I reflect back and see that we've connected at the most perfect times — you introduced me to X at a time in my life that I needed him (and was ready for him) most, you recommended Y who is the most perfect lawyer-match for both my love and I, and now you contact me on the eve of trial. . . no pressure, but let's just say I'm looking forward to connecting with you. . .

And it reminds me, friend, that we are all angels for one another, and we help each other along our life's journey.

64.

"I can see that falling in love with you is a full time job," he said, "It's your gift. And your burden."

"I will devour you," I said, "I'm not nice. I am kind, but I am ferocious."

And because it was dark and we were so close, I could not see his expression.

But I felt him smile, and felt his body relax, and the truth between us was a willing courage that rose like a flame and set fire to the hesitation and uncertainty that had crept into the room, until all that was left was the sound of our breath and yes and yes and yes. . .

65.

And there is a voice that whispers, "Do not miss him," for missing him is a form of hate, of hating that he isn't here and that things are not how they used to be.

To miss him is to collapse into the gap between How It Is Now and How It Was Then – the chasm is deep and jagged, and it hurts to go there.

Sometimes in my mind he Is as he Was: present, attentive, loving.

And then I meet the Now and remember: absent, distracted, disinterested.

At first I tried to Will him back. If only I could be Good Enough, or do the right thing, or wait patiently, or stay silent long enough, maybe he would return and it would be as it was.

And then I tried to Hate him away. If only I could wish upon him the pain I feel, that would make it better.

And then I tried to Erase and Forget him. If only he was nothing to me, as I seem to have become nothing to him.

And then there was a strange measure of Peace that came. That Now is Now. And Then was Beautiful, and the Beauty and lessons learned are mine forever. That perhaps he had but one role to play in my journey, and that was to meet and then to leave.

And yet, from time to time I notice a wistful missing – how nice it was, for a moment.

And I try, now, to turn instead to Appreciation. For I can Appreciate in the Now the qualities I experienced that I adored and loved so much. And I can Appreciate him in the Now for the moments that we shared in the Then.

I can Appreciate without Missing or Longing or Hoping or Hating or Wanting Things to Be Different.

Appreciation is solid ground.

It helps keep me in the Now, in the Present.

It allows for all the other emotions to rise and fall, it makes room for all of it. Without trying to hold on or fight.

I appreciate what I've learned of my heart, and of love.

I appreciate all the ways my pain points the way back to love, and care of self. How it teaches me to hold my heart with tenderness. And teaches me of my own resilience and strength, and courage and willingness.

All of the true things.

66.

Some suffer because they are guarded with love – they hold it back and release very sparingly.

Others suffer because they want to pour it forth, but don't know where to put it or whom to give it.

I feel so full and in flow of Love today because I'm being generous with love – drenching myself with it, sharing it with friends and family and strangers. Sometimes I give a big hug and sometimes it's simply a smile or kind gesture.

Lots of ways for love to move in this world. Feels real good to let it go.

67.

I am on an Artist Date, feeding my creative spirit with color and shape, allowing space to follow my curiosity and pause or look more closely at whatever pleases me – the curve of a lock of hair rendered in marble, or the gold and jeweled ring on the finger of a painted woman, or even the arrangement of roses in a milky blue-green vase on the table in the cafe.

The mind both rests and stretches here. There are new wonders and delights in the artifacts created by others, and though they no longer walk the earth the mark they leave ripples out with great power and gentleness.

The care with which they delivered this beauty to us remains, and continues to contribute to our wellbeing.

Isn't that lovely?

68.

There is a song of joy that I sing whenever I come upon the perfect parking spot. I had cause to sing it just now. The only words in the entire song are "Thank you" and I always imagine a big chorale behind me, and an orchestra, and all of these crescendos and crashing cymbals and bright trumpets.

69.

Curiosity is so powerful – and the good news is that you were born with so much curiosity, it's a natural way for you to be. You already know how.

And: the moment you think you "know" someone and stop being curious about them, well, that's when it becomes really easy to drift apart or let things stagnate. Because we are dynamic creatures, and we are always learning and growing. We discover new dreams, desires, we have all kinds of emotions and thoughts. . . Be curious about those you love. Be open to discover who they are, over and over again.

And, yes, bring this same Curiosity and Kindness to yourself. You might be surprised to discover there's more to you than you realize.

Part 3:

See the love in people.

70.

Oh my loves! And so I boarded the bus with my armload of books and the driver lit up and started to tell me about his daughter, who has loved to read since she was a little girl. "A book a day!" he said, "Can you believe?"

She graduated from Columbia in May and works in DC, and soon she will go to Brazil as a Fulbright scholar. He was just glowing with pride. I even skipped my bus stop to ride a bit longer, to hear more, and be in his presence.

And then I thanked him, and asked his name, and we shook hands and wished each other well.

You can see the love in people.

You never know what will trigger it for them – what will bring up the memory, or the thought that makes them glow.

We're all like the Cave of Wonders in that way. We each have a secret key or phrase that unlocks and opens us, revealing our treasures.

Isn't that so beautiful to know, that all around you are all of these stories and so much love? It's just there. Maybe closer to the surface than you ever could imagine.

71.

Sometimes it is your openness that opens others. It is your love that brings forth love in others.

And sometimes it is the love within others that helps us remember the love we, too, carry within. When others meet us with an open heart, with kindness and curiosity, it invites us to open our heart and to bring our own kindness and curiosity.

So it's important to tend to your own self in this way. And also, to appreciate that sometimes we just need a little help getting jump-started.

72.

Monday morning. Traffic, helicopters, street closures and detours. . . Everyone trying to get to where they're going – sometimes horns honking, sometimes elbows jostled or toes stepped on.

I like the way we look out for each other.

And we will all end up at our final destination, one way or another.

How shall we get there, and what shall we carry? Impatience? Frustration? Curses?

Kindness is lighter. Wonder is lighter. Just for starters.

We each get to choose this for ourselves, over and over again. In any moment, you get to choose.

Today I choose delight and appreciation.

73.

Two things I'm noticing right now.

One, is how much I'm enjoying this quiet rainy day. After a series of days with much out-facing energy flow and holding space for others, a quiet day to be alone and inward is the perfect way to be working. Inhale, exhale. Contract, release. Give, receive.

Two, that Balance isn't "sameness" or "static." It is a relationship, a dynamic flow that allows for variability.

74.

Yes, yes, yes. . . To serendipity, and trains, and rainy nights, and heart soul conversations until quite late, and sunrise, and coffee, and umbrellas, and love, and warm smiles, and sweet dreams, and dear friends, and all of the unplanned beauty that unfolds when you're willing to not plan so hard.

75.

I said, "Slower. . ."

He said, "Yes, baby. . . we can go slow, see how slow I can be with you. . ."

I said, "Can we take a break?"

He said, "Of course, come here and let me just hold you."

I said, "Thank you for this, for everything, for the way you listen, and the way you pay attention to me, and take care of me."

He said, "You are so good for me. Your presence is so calming, so powerful, so feminine. . . You inspire me to worship you."

And then, for a while, there were no words.

There was no need. Just breathing together, holding each other, in the dark.

76.

Wake up with love. Put in contact lenses with love. Drink water with love. Get dressed with love. Put the dishes away with love. Check email with love. Eat an apple with love. Leave the house with love. Walk with love. Ride the bus with love. Enter the room with love.

So much love to bring to life, even at this early hour of the day.

What if you chose to greet the day and all who cross your path with love?

What if your feet meet the ground in every step, with love?

These things are in motion and you are doing them anyway.

And in every moment we have the opportunity to simply go through the motions of living. . . or to infuse our life with love, or kindness, or curiosity, or peace, or whatever quality we choose.

What would you like bring to the moment?

It can be a game.

Today I'm bringing love.

There's so much of it to go around.

And what's really lovely is that whatever you bring – whatever it is that you contribute – be it love or some other quality – is that before you can bring it you first must hold it yourself.

You first must cultivate and carry it.

Be willing to be Love or Kindness or whatever you choose on the inside. Cultivate and carry it and have it for yourself, first – so that you can give to others.

What would you like to cultivate and carry?

You can choose anything.

Today I choose Love.

What will you choose?

77.

Today I saw a friend whom I haven't seen in about 15 years. We drove to meet another mutual friend who is moving to Shanghai.

So it has been a mix of happy and sad in my heart. Happy to have this reunion with a friend – and sad to be sending off another friend to her next chapter.

Life is like that.

It's good to have a big heart, to hold all the Things That Are True.

We can hold Happy and Sad, and all the spaces in between, all at once.

And it is also a reminder to enjoy this moment together. Because we shall never again be together quite the way we are right now.

Sometimes when my heart is full, tears come out of my eyes. Today my heart feels so full. Joy, sadness – it's all Love.

Love love love. . .

And safe travels, to all my friends, and blessings to all of your journeys and every new horizon.

78.

There is a thing that tends to happen when you take care of others, yet do not take care of yourself.

What tends to happen is this thought, "Well, if I take care of others surely someone will notice how much I am caring for them, and then THEY will do things to care for me."

And you're so good, and patiently waiting for someone to care for you, or to just ask how you're doing, or to notice and say, "Wow, you do so much to take care of me – let me now take care of you for a while."

And you wait quietly, because surely they must notice, and any day now, someone will care for you the way you're caring for them.

Maybe years go by.

Maybe they say, "Oh, but I thought you liked doing all the caring, I had no idea you were waiting for me to care for you in that way, too."

Giving feels good, until it feels like a burden.

And then Resentment gathers, slowly, until it becomes heavy and heated.

This is why it is really, really important to take care of yourself.

It is ok to also have needs.

It is ok to say:
"You know, right now I just need a hug." Or,
"I have a need to feel cared for and treated with kindness." Or,
"I would love for someone to make me a cup of tea, or be attentive and listen to me, because that would feel so thoughtful and caring." Or,
"I would like another person to do this part of the caring for today."

We become sustainable Givers when we also Give to ourselves, and Receive for ourselves.

I know a lot about Giving and Waiting Quietly for Someone to Notice and Care. It's a hard and sad place to be, and anger can grow from that place.

I'm better now at Caring for myself all along the way, and also at articulating what I need.

And I've found that very often, people are delighted to give to me! They don't always know how. Especially if I'm always taking on the Giver role.

It's nice to Give and also to Receive. Sometimes the people around us just need an easy and clear invitation, so they know how. They like feeling appreciated for Giving, too.

Giving feels powerful.

But Receiving is powerful, too.

Practice both kinds of power.

79.

And remember that Self-Care doesn't require that you do more things, or even different things. It can simply be about the quality of attention and intention that you bring to that which you already do.

So you can go through the motions of brushing your teeth. Or you can brush your teeth while remembering, "This is one of the ways I take care of myself."

And you can even catch your eye in the mirror and think, "Well hello, friend!" or even, "Well hello, gorgeous!"

If it makes you smile, you're doing it right.

80.

It's raining! I love this rain. Yesterday someone said I smelled good. I told them, "It's the rain."

And they said, "Yeah, but it's something else, too."

And I said, "Oh, that's just me."

And they said, "Yeah," and we smiled.

81.

Emotions are powerful. That's why I say, "I'm feeling powerful" instead of "I'm feeling emotional." People get really weird about emotions.

And sometimes, when I have certain emotions – frustration, or anger, for example – a person will try to explain things, like, "Oh, well, I was just trying to. . ." It's an interesting dynamic and I've noticed it with many different people – sometimes it feels like a defensive move, like, "If only I explain things MORE then she'll stop having emotions at me."

And what's interesting is that I can be feeling the emotion and yet speaking really calmly – "I'm noticing that I feel really angry" – and the Explaining starts, which feels disrespectful.

I'm realizing this is also why I've spent so many years *hiding* emotions or trying to *not have* certain emotions (it doesn't work, in case you were wondering!). Because so often it seemed to create distance, misunderstanding, and a feeling of being disrespected or perceived as not smart for having them.

Oh! And, insight: I realize that so many years and so much energy have been put into trying to prove that I'm smart. So it's extra scary to do anything that looks not-smart – like having emotions, because, clearly, if I really understood then I wouldn't have those emotions. That's why he explains over and over again, more loudly and more insistent. He feels so misunderstood, and treated unfairly (maybe, I don't actually know what he feels).

This is a thing.

It's a bit like the weather. Once I can see the pattern, I can stop taking it personally. It's also a Thing That Happens.

No wonder.

So, my Powerful Ones, you can have emotions around me, I know what it's like. And I'm ok with you having them.

And I'm ok with having emotions, too. I'm learning to work with this power. It feels really good.

82.

Sometimes when you have emotions near someone, they will feel attacked, or as if they are being accused of failure or wrong-doing.

Or, they may feel so uncomfortable in the presence of your emotions – they may want to fix or help.

They may try to explain your emotions away, or become defensive.

Humans are not always skillful with the power of emotions, and this true of their own and yours, too.

Don't let it get you down.

You are always allowed to feel your feels. Let emotions come and go.

You don't need to explain them, or justify them, or use them as fuel for action.

You can just notice: "Oh, right now I have a lot of emotion. I have _____, and _____, and even a little _____."

83.

The hard thing about hard conversations is that they are hard.

But the great thing is that when you are willing to have them, you don't carry the burden, or let the ouch turn into a resentment.

So don't be afraid because they are hard, or because your face feels hot and your voice feels shaky. Try this – take a deep breath to help calm and steady your body. Then say the words – be kind to yourself, and allow for uncertainty.

Sometimes it feels messy and scary. It's ok.

Try it and see what happens.

This is especially hard if you're the kind of person who is accustomed to just sucking it up, keeping silent, and ignoring things in order to keep the peace. Also hard if you tend to process on the inside, later – because your instinct is to be quiet and get out of the stressful situation, until you feel safe to process.

So it might not be *easy* exactly, but it can be so healing and strengthening – to allow the hard conversation, right there, in the moment.

I think we build strength in our wings this way.

Freedom is having a hard conversation.

Prison is carrying a resentment, holding your words inside, and replaying over and over again what you could or should have said, but didn't.

84.

Today I meditate in the garden. I don't know the name of these blossoms, but they are so fragrant!

When the roses are sleeping through winter and offer only their magnificent brambles and thorns, stop to smell the cluster of white flowers on the green stalks. If you are lucky, there will be beautiful red berries scattered on the ground nearby.

85.

The year was amazing for my Heart – breaks and aches, and discovering new depths and courage and tenderness. Feeling deeply loved, and also, at times, very alone and very sad.

And as I consider the year behind, I ask my Heart, "How are you?"

And my Heart laughs and says, "Strong, and open, and full!"

86.

Your Heart is good and strong.

You are a Feeling Creature – Sensitive and Sensual – and these are Marvelous and Powerful aspects of being a Human.

Love to you, my Beloved One – today, tonight, and all Days and all Nights.

87.

I'm at a cafe, sipping coffee that someone else has made for me. It occurs to me how normal this is – and when I look back on the year and think of all the services and care I've received from others along the way. It's astonishing.

So: Thank you to those who work behind the scenes to make life amazing.

All who help to prepare the space, who make the food, who serve the coffee, who refill the water glass, who have things in place at just the right time, who tidy up, who are thoughtful to the needs of others – and who are often unseen and unacknowledged.

And also, to all those who are on the front lines, who face a long line of demanding, frazzled, tired, and short-tempered customers and travelers. It's not an easy job, and the grace and steadiness you bring are often overlooked as people speed through on their way somewhere else.

I don't always see you, but I know you're there.

I see the power of your work. You have my gratitude, appreciation, and respect.

Thank you for taking care of me, and all of us.

88.

There is a quieting this time of year, a kind of collective breath and sigh as we begin to release one year and reach for the next.

It's an amazing thing to be alive. We forget to notice the little wonders of daily life, we've become so accustomed to them.

Fortunately, we are surrounded by reminders. Children. Animals. Nature.

Just look up, from time to time. Look at the sky. Allow yourself a moment of stillness to take in the magnificence all around you.

89.

I've been quiet. Sometimes that is the best way to be. It's easier to listen when you're quiet, and then you can notice and hear things that you would have otherwise missed. Quiet and slow. . . there is a luxurious brilliance about them, especially at this time of year.

Love to the quiet ones, and to those who take their time.

90.

When you understand the elemental dynamics of a person – when you observe and notice their patterns and cadence – then you don't take it personally, any more than you take the rain personally. They are their own weather, and they are on their own path.

Remembering this makes it possible to appreciate them, while also being more deliberate and intentional about how you wish to relate to them. Bring an umbrella, or simply appreciate them from a safe and sheltered distance.

91.

My heart feels so full. My feet feel so connected to the Earth. My spirit feels so expansive.

If you are reading this, then know that you are already a part of this magic. I will always offer words – and if you are reading then you are receiving them, sipping them with your eyes and letting the warmth and love percolate at some level of your being.

We are in this together. This has been true for a while.

The only thing we decide is the shape and terms.

The closeness is already here.

What could be closer than this.

Words to carry the energy, love, delight.

Words like a hand to hold in the dark, when it's difficult.

Words to connect us on our journey.

You and me.

I'm glad you're here.

92.

Sometimes the living truth of being mindful in the world looks like this.

I go to LGA and flights are being cancelled and delayed due to poor visibility. I'm feeling stressed, anxious about my flights and connections, trying to juggle things with the airline rep on the phone.

I go to the agent at my gate and as I approach I'm thinking: "I'm glad you're here!" and "This is a person who can help me."

I'm wanting to show up with an internal tone of warmth and curiosity and kindness – rather than being an irritated, frazzled, demanding traveler.

What I tell her is: "My flight's delayed, and I'll miss my connection. How do I get to SFO tonight?"

I'll be honest – there was a part of me that was feeling pissy and wanted to just say, "What will you do to FIX THIS???" – but that's not how I wanted to present or show up.

So.

She's very patient and looking at my boarding passes and her screen and trying to sort things out so I can get home tonight. It's all looking terrible – will take 3 planes and it could so easily fall apart.

Then she looks up at me and says, "What about Kennedy? There's a flight direct to SFO at 5pm."

I have no idea how feasible that is, and it feels ridiculous to be AT AN AIRPORT and being told to go to ANOTHER airport. What? My stressed brain cannot process this.

She says, "We can't pay for the cab, but it will take about 40 minutes."

I'm listening. I'm really, really listening.

And what I hear is: *This woman really is doing her best to help you.* Am I willing to receive it?

She says, "It's three planes or one plane. I'm trying to save you the trouble of three planes."

I take a deep breath. She's right.

"Ok," I say, "You are wise. Let's do it."

She starts typing – fast fast fast – and says with confidence and satisfaction, "I've been doing this a long time!"

Suddenly it feels like we are in this together.

She says, "You check any bags?"

"No! Just carry on."

"Thatta girl."

She hands me my new boarding pass.

She says, "You're all set. You can go straight to the gate."

She gives me directions to find the cab stand. I do this, and the nicest cabbie whisks me away in a bright yellow cab!

I get to JFK. The line to get through security is FOREVER long.

A guy is saying, "Check your boarding pass – if it says TSA Pre-check, step to this other line."

I look at my boarding pass, and it says TSA PRECHK – and so I whoosh by the crowd and in 2 minutes I'm through security.

Hooray!

And this is part of the beauty of this practice: of taking a deep breath, of carrying "I'm glad you're here" on the inside of yourself, of being willing to listen deeply.

Unexpected things will happen – like weather, and cancelled flights.

And people will have the power to help you.

And the way you listen can change the way things go.

It can change the way people are willing to show up for you because it changes how YOU show up for THEM. And it changes the way you hear things – so you can receive help that you might have brushed off before.

My flight is due to arrive SFO at 8:47pm, which is 3 hours earlier than the 3-plane option.

I'm feeling grateful, relaxed, and very fortunate.

93.

And you wake up, and look outside, and the sky is ravishing – this brilliant and breathtaking slow movement of color – and there is so much beauty it's more than a picture can hold, more than your eyes can hold, more than your heart can hold.

And the only thing to do is to open and open and open and let it wash over you and soak beauty and joy into your very bones.

94.

Sun slips away, beautiful day,
Lovely the sky and the sea.
Evening descends, as the day ends,
Over the ocean and me.

95.

For the meditation lovers, the mindfulness people – a few great places to stress-test your practice, to see what happens when there's a little heat or friction – Work. Airports. Family.

Sitting practice is like being in the studio. It's lovely to practice in the studio. How charming, how fun! And where we need the skill of being present, centered, and calm is in the field, in the uneven and unpredictable terrain of an active life.

96.

The highs and lows will always be part of life. We don't get to be in control.

"If I do everything right, then things will go my way and I'll get what I want. I'll get all the ups and none of the downs."

It doesn't work like that, love.

We're humans. We bump up against each other, and sometimes step on each others toes.

It's part of the dance.

How much energy you put into it is your thing, not theirs.

How you heal it is your thing, not theirs.

Apologize when you need to apologize, and be ok knowing that not everyone will do the same.

Keep dancing.

And have fun.

97.

Good morning, love. And how will you attend to your own self-care today?

Perhaps by showing up for your meditation practice.
Perhaps by having a difficult conversation.
Perhaps by drinking a glass of water.
Perhaps by accepting a compliment without first trying to deflect it or make it small.
Perhaps by enjoying the clarity that comes from uncomfortable situations.

Perhaps by giving the small-child version of you, on the inside, a hug and saying, "I love you, and I'm glad you're here."

98.

My roommate just asked me if I had a morning ritual of affirmations – anything I always said to myself upon waking up.

"No," I said, "But I do have this. . . "

And I showed her my alarms.

6:30am: Good morning beautiful!
7:00am: Rise and shine, my love!
7:17am: Wake up honey, it's good to be alive.

She started laughing and said that it counts.

99.

There is a heartache that is deeper than this one boy.

The emotions reach back, beyond the time we have known one another.

Something familiar, from long ago. A similar ache.

20 years – or perhaps 2,000.

"I know you," I say, "I remember you from before."

It asks: Will you love me? Will you hold me?

I say: Yes.

Before, I had tried to cut out the ache and throw it away. I had tried to tamp it down, to quiet or numb it, or reason it away. I had tried to run.

Tonight, I say: Yes.

It crawls up into my arms and rests against my heart.

The heartache does not go away, exactly, but somehow it's held with such tenderness and care that its presence only points to wholeness and unconditional love.

Be willing to love.

Be willing to be at peace with your pain.

And should there be tears, let them be a washing, a healing, for your own tender heart.

Part 4:

Be willing to love.

100.

Be willing to love – right now – just as it is, just as you are.

Notice the ways you already make a difference in this world. In the life of even one person – even to smile at a stranger, or to offer someone your seat on the bus. To put the socks away. The small domestic things.

These may be small things, but they add up and they ripple out – in ways you will never fully see or appreciate.

Your love and your influence are immeasurable.

Be willing to love. Right now.

Your love might seem small, like a grain of sand, or a flickering tea light, or a single flower, or a gentle ripple.

And the ocean and the world might seem so big, so stormy, that this little love doesn't seem to matter.

It matters, my love. More than you will ever know.

Just as it is.

Just as you are.

Right now –

Be willling to love.

101.

Being willing to listen deeply means you listen beneath the words. It can make all the difference in the world.

102.

There are layers, my love. Listen deeply.

Remember that your willingness to be present to the fullness of another is a beautiful gift. It is a gift that nourishes our heart and spirit – feeling seen for all of who we are – and also connects us, one to the other.

And remember that "to be present" means a willingness to see and accept without putting your opinions or advice all over them.

"Oh, you feel angry. Let me tell you what worked for me. . ."
"Oh, you feel sad. Here's what I do when I feel that way. . ."

Wait, love. Not yet.

First:

See how being present and holding space for all that is becomes the gift of unconditional acceptance.

Practice listening to all the layers, my love.

It's like this.

Words – listen to the words they use.

Sound –- listen to the sound of their voice, the tone, the volume, the warmth or chop of it. This can point to Emotions and that which lies beneath the words.

Emotions 1.0 – listen for the emotional tone beneath the words. There will be clues in the tone of voice, in the sound that carries the words. Also clues in the body.

Emotions 2.0 – listen for YOUR emotional response. This can point to the emotion coming from the other, because we are wired for empathy and so can feel what others feel. When you notice that you yourself are having an emotion, get quiet inside and see if you can sense if it is *your* emotion or if you are mirroring the emotion of the person before you.

Body Language – notice the shape of their body, notice movement, notice how they hold themselves, is their body tense or relaxed.

If it seems like a lot, you can just practice with one layer at a time.

But do practice.

This is how we become more present for each other.

Wouldn't that be a lovely way to be?

103.

I have a lot of emotions. Sometimes they come out of my eyes. Joy, anger, heartache. . . I feel all these, and more.

It gets very intense sometimes.

Emotions can be very inconvenient.

Sometimes I put them away for later and then forget about them.

They never forget about me, though.

They tug at my hem – Now? How about now? Is it time now?

Shhh, I say, *soon*.

That only works for so long.

They need to move. They need to have their say. They need to be allowed to be here, too.

There are some emotions I'm very familiar with, and feel quite good at having.

And there are other emotions I'm only on nodding terms with, I feel very uncertain and clumsy with them.

I am an Emotional Creature.

You are, too.

Aren't we lucky?

104.

Lovely, lovely rain. I love the sound of it, and the way the air tastes. I love how everything feels cozy. I love how the colors look different – the blur and shine of them.

105.

Noticing how "alone" is actually pretty close to "all one" – and that's what intimacy feels like, that closeness where you feel at one with another.

And it leads me to consider. . .

What if feeling alone is a forgetting of how you are all-one, intimately connected, already? What if it's a reminder of the absence of separateness – a reminder of *closeness*.

Isn't that neat?

Sometimes I feel alone in a lonely kind of way, and the feels that come with it are Sad and Shame and Confused.

What if those feels could signal me back to All-One, to feeling Intimate, Connected, Close, Loved, Held. What if it was even more close than Couple or Together.

What if Alone looped around to We? We still implies More Than One, which implies Space and Distance.

Which can be Lovely in their own right, of course.

Anyway.

I love you.

106.

Be willing to extend the same kindness to yourself as you would a dear friend. When a friend is lost, you extend a hand and gently lead them back. You don't yell at them or hurt them with your words.

It's the same with refocusing when you feel stuck, stalled, or derailed. You simply notice, and bring yourself back with kindness.

107.

You have a Physical body. It needs nourishment, movement, and rest.

Choose to care for your Physical body as if it were a good friend.

Notice what you appreciate about it, and tell it that it's dear to you.

Say "Hello friend" to your face when you see yourself in the mirror.

Admire your hands, and all that they carry, and all that they do.

Enjoy your ears, and all that they hear.

Smile to your own mouth, for the words it can speak.

Thank your feet for all the steps they take.

108.

It's almost Halloween! And so I'm thinking a lot about identity and candy – the sweet surprises that we receive when we play with our idea of who we are and who we might be.

What happens when we get friendly with the monster and angel and animal and playful and sexy and scary sides to our self?

It feels a little risky – Trick or Treat? – but this is the time to take such risks, ask such questions, play with how you show up and ring a stranger's doorbell.

109.

There was one night, on the island, when my friend and I climbed into the hammock (it is a big hammock!) that hangs between two trees in an open space, away from the buildings and lights.

And it was night, so the stars were out. And there were no clouds and few lights, so the stars were bright, and so many!

I don't know when I've seen so many stars.

And I looked and looked and looked, and I decided to soak up as much starlight as I possibly could.

Living in the city, it's not often that I get to soak up starlight. But right now, I'm feeling quite brilliant with it.

110.

My work is quiet work.

It is the unseen, and the undeniable.

It is felt in the body, and the heart. The mind releases its grip and opens to wonder.

And sometimes it is difficult to appreciate the value of quiet work in a world that measures and counts only that which is easily rendered into numerical form and placed upon a bottom line.

Sometimes we forget that Science is a way of seeing, it is observation – and that numbers are but one tool with which we attempt to render, or translate, or share that which is observed.

Just as a sound wave may be described in visual form, in numeric form. A musical note may be represented by shapes on a staff. They are not the sound itself. They are not the experience of the sound. They are only a representation of it, a way of describing it.

That which is observed, the mind may muddle as it applies its own meaning and interpretation. The mind has its own set of lenses, which filter and shape observation to understanding.

Devotion is willingness to continue the quiet work, in a noisy world. Devotion helps you find stillness and strength, focus and forward momentum, even when you feel discouraged. Devotion is love by your side, saying *Yes, my love.*

Devotion reminds you that even if you can't quite see the path, feel it beneath your feet and continue, one step at a time.

If your work is also quiet work, remember this and be encouraged.

111.

Sometimes the Start is the hardest part.

There's so much to learn! So much to do! What if I start wrong? What if it doesn't work?

My friend. . .

What if it's amazing?
What if learning is more valuable than being right?
What if it's ok to have more questions than answers?

Just start, love.

112.

It has rained every day.

Each morning, a drop-drop-drop-VOOOSH of rain.
Every evening, a pitter-patter-SHOOOOM of rain.

A few drops slow, then a torrential downpour for about 10 minutes, then it tapers again and is over.

It's wonderful.

113.

Deep breath and big sigh. . . I was in the ocean having a magical conversation with my friend when I suddenly felt a sharp stab near the heel of my left foot. Very startling and so painful. Best guess is I set my foot upon a sea urchin, but we're not sure. (Sorry sea urchin!)

It's getting better, and I'm being very gentle with it. We shall keep an eye on it.

I am grateful for a body that is so sensitive, and so good at healing.

I am happy to have my friend with me, and grateful to be a guest on this beautiful island.

And right now I am sending love and holding a vision of whole health and vitality for all who are in pain.

I am also sending a blessing to all sea urchins. May they live in peace, without humans accidentally stepping on them.

114.

The sun will be hot, your feet may slip, you will sweat, you will feel your strong heart beat. Take just one step at a time. And drink in the view, replenish your spirit, and celebrate this being alive – the whole of it – the heat, sweat, and stumbling that comes with choosing to embark upon such a journey.

115.

Not as you expected, and not quite the way you planned. And also, absolutely perfect.

116.

"The first time I met you," she said, "I was kind of intimidated. You're so. . . tall, and you have all this glorious hair, and the person I was talking to saw you and lit up. . ."

"Oh really? Because the first time I met YOU," I said, "I felt kind of intimidated, too! You're so cool, and stylish, and you just have this way about you that made me feel like country mouse, like I just was not going to be cool enough to hang out with you. . ."

And then we started laughing.

"And now I feel safe with you because you've seen me cry."

"Yeah, you've seen me cry, too. You've seen me be messy. I don't feel like I have to be together all the time."

"I feel that way, too."

Oh my friends, isn't it interesting? How it is when we first meet each other, and then we get to a place of feeling comfortable with ourselves and each other?

Isn't it a relief to know it's ok to be a human, and to have all the emotions, and to be with people who can see you cry and still be your friend? Who can laugh with you, too, until your face hurts?

I don't love you because you're perfect. I love you because you're human.

I don't love us because we never have conflict, or misunderstandings. I love us because we have those things and we are still good.

117.

In this morning's session these words arrived: "We close our eyes so we can see better."

Sometimes we close our eyes to become more present to the moment – to what our physical body is sensing, to what emotions are moving within us, to what thoughts are playing across our mind.

Sometimes it helps to close eyes so that you can more easily notice what's beneath the surface – so you can tune in to and see what's there.

118.

This year I've been practicing my No's and my Yes-es. That means, I've been practicing giving true No's and Yes-es, even with simple things and even when it feels uncomfortable.

Tonight I was in conversation with a few members of the team about an event we are hosting tomorrow. One person asked me if I'd take care of X.

I said No.

She said, "You know, I'm glad you said that. I know that I've been asking a lot from you. And now I know that you'll say No if it's No. And that you won't just say Yes all the time. So, thank you."

Isn't that wonderful? I said No, and my colleague feels even more sure of me, and trusting of me. And I'm feeling more relaxed, too, because I'm taking care of myself – and not just throwing out a string of careless and over-committed Yes-es.

Sometimes we say Yes or No because we are trying to manage the other person's response. We want them to like us, so we say Yes or No. We want to avoid conflict so we say Yes or No.

Learning to say Yes or No from the gut – in a simple way, without layers of anger or fear or extra emotions – this is something that is good to practice. It is good to practice in small ways, with small things, so that when the big things come up you already are in the habit of answering from that true place, in an easy way.

119.

Oh, this: Attend to the How.

How are you being? How are you setting forth with the list of doings?

I'm noticing many become overwhelmed or lost in the What. What to do? Too many to dos! What to focus on first?

I'm noticing many reflect and connect to the Why – it ignites a passion, it inspires a vision, it creates a sense of urgency and purpose that can energize and attract others to the work.

And then, I'm noticing that for many, the How is heavy on anxiety, fear, urgency, impatience, loudness, and self-neglect. The How is infused with a frenetic buzzing, sometimes there is a kind of numbness or blindness that is depleting, or abrasive to self and others.

"But it's normal. It's just how I am. It's just how things are."

That is a costly choice.

The Why is fuel and vision and purpose. It reaches to Past and Future.

Yes and good.

But the How is Now.

If the How is impatient, combative, unkind, careless, and callous, then we contribute unkindness, combativeness, carelessness, and callousness.

It doesn't help.

How are you Being?

Be kind, friends.

Be curious.

Be a friend to yourself.

Be compassionate.

Be relaxed and clear and joy-filled.

As we attend to and cultivate these in our life, we each benefit immediately. And so do all those around us.

Isn't it lovely?

120.

My nephew is 13 months old, and beautiful, with chubby little cheeks and a smile to melt your heart. He reminds me of what it is like to be new to the world, figuring out the walking and talking, learning new things every day.

On the bus tonight there was a man who was not well – ranting about cell phones and society and women, and saying unkind things in a loud voice.

And perhaps on another day I would have felt very uncomfortable, or irritated by this.

But tonight. . . it occurred to me that there was a time, many years ago, when he, too, was new to the world – beautiful, with chubby little cheeks, and a smile to melt your heart.

I hope that someone held him, and comforted him, and loved him the way my nephew is held, comforted, and loved.

For now people only want to be away from him.

But it probably wasn't always like that.

Love to all the lost ones, the staggering and ranting ones.

121.

How is there room for more projects?

It's a bit like being a lighthouse, I think. Keep centered, attend to the source light within, and add new lenses to reach more people.

Sometimes devotion means being still, and tending that source light, and polishing the lens so that it may shine more clearly and reach further more easily.

122.

There is always more happening beneath the surface than you realize. We are all such magnificent icebergs, such vast oceans.

123.

And walking home, feeling the fog on my face, feeling quiet inside, I come upon a series of friends – all are wearing soft, fuzzy, warm sweaters – and so I receive a series of soft, fuzzy, warm hugs!

Which is exactly what I was wanting right now.

Thank you, good and generous world.

124.

Afraid to look.

It started in July. My laptop went dark. I plugged it in, and it started, but would not hold a charge. It no longer recognized the battery.

"I'll just work around this," I thought. I'll just stay plugged in always.

I was afraid to look. Afraid of the cost and time to repair. It was easier to stay plugged to the wall and rearrange my life.

Until last week. When suddenly, I needed to be able to be mobile.

I couldn't hide it anymore. I couldn't ignore it anymore.

I talked to my friend. She said, "Go to the Apple Store. See what they can do."

I felt nervous but I did. They said, "Let's make an appointment."

My appointment was today. I was scared of what would happen. I was afraid of the cost. Of how much time it would take.

He ran a diagnostic.

He said the battery needed to be replaced. They had it in stock. It would be a day or two. $137 or so.

I felt my whole body relax and I smiled. That's not so bad at all! I wish I'd handled this months ago!

Why did I wait so long?

Why did I wait until I was really in a bind?

Isn't it fascinating?

We all do this.

We are afraid to look.

We are afraid to find out – what if it's bad? I'd rather work hard at not looking.

Oh, my love.

This is a common thing.

Afraid to look at big things and small things. Because, what then?

If I really look, what then?

Money. Relationships. Career. Life. The check engine light on your dashboard. That little twinge in your side. The unopened letter.

Take a breath. Step toward discomfort and the unknown.

Today I'm feeling relief about my laptop, and am wondering what else I'm not looking at.

And I'm sending so much love and compassion for those who are Afraid to Look.

125.

Love can be steady, but not static.

Relationships are dynamic, not fixed.

Devotion is not sameness, but willingness. As such, it allows for variety. The cadence and form may shift. Constraints may inspire creativity. This does not diminish love.

I am devoted to you, my love, in ways that are not always evident. Your inability to notice them does not diminish their presence or effect.

When you are distracted, I am here. All you need is to remember to look for me, and you shall find me here, beside you as always, closer than close, devoted to your deepest well-being and greatest ambition.

126.

Conversation inside my head:

"Crystals? Really? You believe in that stuff?"

"I believe in Beauty, and in Nature."

"Yeah. Me, too."

127.

Sometimes I get caught in a "not enough" storm.

It goes like this:
"I'm not doing enough" or
"I'm not working enough" or
"I'm not meditating enough" or
"I'm not focused enough" or
"I'm not productive enough" or
"I'm not drinking water enough" or
"I'm not writing enough" or
"I'm not playing enough"
etc, etc.

It's an interesting place to be. Kind of like being in a dusty whirlwind – difficult to see, a kind of grit and heat and sting, a sense of frenzy that won't settle down.

It's a comparison place – looking outward, and comparing to others – and looking inward with judgmental eye that does not help – and even though I KNOW one shouldn't I still have a tendency to do this from time to time.

We humans are like this, I think.

There's a bit of fear in it. A bit of frustration and anger, too.

The way I've been handling it lately is like this:

Noticing the frenetic conversation on the inside of my mind.

Saying, "Oh, hey there. I know you. We know each other."

I listen, it says, "not enough, not enough, not enough. . ."

I say, "Oh yeah? Well, what if that wasn't actually true? And what if it's exactly as it should be in this moment. And what happens if you look around at all the enoughness and see how enough it is, and how enough you are?"

And I hear, "Really? Could that be so?"

And I say, "Shall we find out?"

And I hear, ". . . . Ok."

And then we practice enoughness. We practice noticing it, and feeling it. And it feels good.

It's like a cool rain that calms and soothes the dust storm, settles the heat and sting of it. It's like a glass of water on a hot day.

I'm getting better at being a friend to myself.

This makes it easier to share more of myself with others.

There is so much to share, friends.

Plenty.

More than enough.

128.

Sometimes the most kind, healing, loving thing to say is: "I didn't realize you felt that way. Thank you for telling me."

Sometimes we become so devoted to our own world view that we can't imagine any possible alternative. We hold our view as "right" and others as "wrong."

Sometimes I say, "I am feeling ____." And the person says, "Well, you shouldn't." Or, "That doesn't make sense." Or, "Well, let me explain why I did this or said this, and then you will understand."

The explaining is like a beating.

"I have opinions about what you are feeling – listen to my right-ness of them." Ouch.

Offering words around an emotional experience — "I feel. . ." – can require such courage, and can be scary, as we put out into the open the most tender parts of ourself.

"I didn't realize you felt that way. Thank you for telling me."

Say it with kindness in your bones. Perhaps, feel honored that this person chose to share something so personal.

"I didn't realize you felt that way. Thank you for telling me."

This builds trust. This builds a bridge. This connects.

It is beyond blame. It is beyond justification or defense.

Let's meet there, please.

129.

I have started to notice more silvery strands in the mix of brown, red, and gold in my hair. I love this. It's like having moonlight in my hair, all the time.

130.

Sometimes I want someone to be a certain way and when they are not, I feel really disappointed and angry.

I had a moment of bright clarity on this a little while ago.

I felt so angry! So disappointed! How could this person be like that? Why were they doing this to me?

And a voice inside said, "Why are you so upset?"

And I answered, "Because this person isn't the way I want them to be!"

And there was a pause. . . and then: Oh. Oops. I see.

And then this question: "Can you be ok with someone, exactly as they are?"

And I really had to sit with that, like untangling a necklace by being very gentle at tugging different sides of the knot to find out how to release it.

And I answered, "But I want people to be the way I want them to be."

And then, "Yes, love, I know. And do you see how this makes things so difficult for you?"

And I worked a bit more on my tangled necklace, and I saw how it was true.

And I answered, "Yes, I see."

And then, "And do you see how you take things so personally, when maybe this person is just being who they are? And maybe they are doing the best they can?"

And I answered, "Yes, I think so."

I'm not always good at remembering this lesson. So I'm writing it down, in hopes that by doing so I will remember.

Part 5:

Relax so that love can happen.

131.

I had coffee and a pecan roll, and my journal. There were just a few tables, and a woman with coffee and scone sat across from me. We made eye contact and half-smiled, acknowledging each other.

A few minutes pass and she says, "Is your birthday in August?"

"Yes," I say, "You noticed my pendant."

"Yeah," she says, "It's a peridot. My birthday is in August, too."

And very gently, the words begin to come. We begin to chat, and then:

"Relax so that love can happen," she says, "That's what my Marcelo taught me. I lost him too soon. We had five years together. I lost him four months ago. There was an accident. He fell off a roof. I still have his cowboy hat."

And there was a feeling of such tenderness, and kindness, and love, and when the tears begin to come we both let them fall. It was beautiful and tender and raw.

And I feel that all of the emotion I've felt in the last week – all of the tears and turbulence – helped me because it allowed me to be calm and love-connected in the presence of her tears and turbulence. It allowed me to feel and listen, and be comfortable with her emotions.

We were able to be together – strangers in a bakery – in our own little world, for a moment, in which love and grief flowed.

"You're very sweet," she said, "What's your name?"

And I stood and we exchanged names, and we hugged and laughed.

And then she had to go, and so we parted.

Friends, relax so that love can happen.

132.

Remember that serendipity offers many gifts, and so be prepared to receive un-planned for delights. Enjoy this life and all the uncertainty that comes with the journey.

We are each a gift unto each other.

133.

Yesterday this realization landed like a bolt of lightning through the core of my being: I love solving Puzzles! I loathe solving Problems.

When something is presented as a Puzzle, I feel curious, open, engaged, playful, and I want to get into it and see if I can find a way for the pieces to fit with one another in a harmonious and delightful fashion.

When something is presented as a Problem, I feel a sense of foreboding, resistance, sometimes sadness or sluggish reluctance – I fidget under the framework that things are "broken" and need to be fixed, and I also notice an anxiety because I think of problems like math problems – where there is only one solution and so many ways to get it wrong.

This little mindset shift has been working its magic on me the last day or so. Realizing that I like solving Puzzles has made me reconsider how I'm looking at so many things! I'm asking new questions, like:

- What are all the pieces?

- How might they fit?

- Do I seem to have all the pieces, or am I missing some?

- How many ways are there to look at the pieces – turn

them over, flip them around, slide them close or apart
to see how things look now. . .

Puzzles feel inviting and engaging.

Problems feel burdensome and exhausting.

Even the very word, "Puzzle," has this lovely little buzzzzz in it.
Very energizing.

So, I'm doing my best to approach challenges as Puzzles, rather
than Problems. It's a small thing – like shifting the point of
leverage the tiniest bit.

Yet it's making such a big difference – as levers do.

134.

Today was a good day, though it started out a bit rough – lots
of emotions, and tears, and feeling so many things.

I'm not always good at asking for help, or reaching out to friends
to tell them when I need some love.

There's a part of me that feels like I should be able to handle it on my
own – that I should just get over it – that I'm making a big deal out of
nothing – that I don't want to bother people with my problems and
feels afraid it will seem like I'm fishing for compliments.

But today I feel like I did a good job of reaching out for help.

And in case you are also a person who tends to isolate when you hit a rough patch, and is still learning how to ask for support, I want to share with you the exact process and words that I used, which got me un-stuck and connected to my community.

The message structure was this:

- How I'm feeling.
- What I'm wanting.
- A clear ask for help.

I texted a few friends – text because it's quick and light, and I know my people are likely to have phones close by and would be able to respond easily.

The message I sent was this:

My heart hurts right now and I feel very sad. I'm wanting a kind word of encouragement or love. Can you help?

And my friends took such good care of me!

Notes of love, offers to come over for tea and hugs, phone calls – a very sweet and gentle rain of love, encouragement, and acceptance to soothe me and help me feel connected and cared for.

And it helped so much, and I'm feeling so much better.

I'm a lucky girl, and a much loved girl, and also very human
Even though I know I'm cared for, that everything is going to
be ok – sometimes I still feel very sad or hurt or lonely, and it
helps to allow my friends to know this and to love me.

If any of this resonates with you, I hope that sharing this story
helps.

And big big love and gratitude to those who were with me today,
in thought, text, Skype, or in person, loving and accepting me
when I felt so sad. I feel centered and happy again.

135.

Here is an experiment I'm trying today: "What if, just for today,
you decided to not take anything personally?"

I'm curious to see what happens.

136.

FAIL = F*ck yeAh, I'm Learning!

I'm smiling so big because I'm having the BEST FAILs. This
year, if you knew how many things did not go according to plan,

or unravelled along the way, or came out all wonky and different than what I thought it would be going in. . .

And, to be honest, sometimes it feels so sucky and sad and frustrating.

But you know, I think this is the whole point! This is what happens when you live out and test things, rather than running non-stop mental simulations on the inside. . .

This idea that feedback is valuable – F*ck yeAh, I'm Learning – I wonder if this is how dolphins feel, sending out all this signal, non-stop, and what bounces back tells them about the world and where they are in it.

This is so good.

And if you're in it, too, then you know that it also really helps to keep a sense of humor, and to not take yourself so seriously.

Big belly laughs and super big hugs to you, my friends, and all the ways you're showing up, putting yourself out there, and dancing with Life.

137.

This lovely day! Like gold in the sky, and this gorgeous expanse of blue stretched out before me.

I love the seamless arc of blue and pink and gold above – how it moves, the most gentle flourish as morning unfurls and offers itself and says, "Here, for you. Enjoy."

138.

Today: opening to new depths of Exquisite Self-Care, and allowing Intuition to guide me.

Today: not fighting or arguing or rationalizing or shaming my emotions.

Today: listening to and believing the Wisdom within.

And redrawing the map of my universe, noting the presence, absence, trajectory, and orbit of those who appear (and disappear) from my sky.

139.

Inspiration hangover. And wondering, too, if the obsession around "solving a problem" is creating a tendency to look out across the world and see nothing but problems. Be careful, or your mind will get stuck there and believe what it sees. And that is the worst kind of confinement.

Is there room for not wanting to solve problems?

Is there room for wanting to nourish and grow and explore and create – absent a problem-solving function?

Is there room to not scale? Is there room for intimacy and limited immediate range?

Is there room for exalted rest, for going slow, for something that is both exquisite and exalted precisely because of this nature?

I think the answer must be Yes, because the world seems big enough for all possibilities, including these.

As a practical matter, I am still learning what this looks like.

140.

I've come upon a very sweet little park in my neighborhood, tucked away with trees like sentinels and a population of brilliant flowers, green vines tumbling amongst each other, bees bumbling from bloom to blossom, and butterflies tripping lightly along an unseen path.

Everyday magic, my loves.

And a reminder that sanctuary may be closer than you think.

141.

I've taken myself out on a little adventure. It's a place I've never been before, but have wanted to visit.

I have my journal and a glass of white wine and a very fine view of the city.

I am eavesdropping on those around me, writing stories in my journal, and sketching ideas for retreats and classes.

We are on a date, my heart and I.

And while there are many things I know, many adventures I've had – still, these matters of the heart vex me most.

Love to all the disheartened ones, the single lovers, and courage and comfort to all those tending a skittish heart.

142.

The sweetness of "Yes, And. . ." is that it makes room for all the emotions, thoughts, and versions of yourself that could possibly exist. And sometimes these cycle through me like a storm.

A friend writes to me and says, "I hope you've been well – from your Facebook page it definitely looks like things are good."

Yes, And. . . these last few days my heart has felt so needy and insecure.

Talking with my dad yesterday, he says, "You know, sometimes I think you keep things too close. It's hard to help you if you don't talk about what you need."

Yes, And. . . he's right, and it doesn't make it any easier to put words around it, because as soon as I do I start crying.

A friend who read an advance copy of my book tells me:

"I loved the book! So beautiful – literally every page was beautiful. I cried multiple times (in the best way possible!). I felt like you literally leapt off the pages a few times, and whispered lovely things in my ears. So delightful and wonderful. I will write a proper full review shortly, but I wanted you to know how truly grateful I was for your work, and how much I enjoyed it and love you!"

Yes, And. . . what's next? What project comes next?

So it's a funny thing – feeling excited, scared, loved, abandoned, appreciated, angry, lost, powerful, helpless, triumphant. . . All of these things. All the time. Like an electrical storm.

The sweetness of "Yes, And. . ." is that it makes room for ALL of this, for all of me. When I fear that I'm Too Much, or Not Enough, when I feel old wounds flare up, or a Shame Spiral gather and begin to pull me down, the only thing that holds it all is Yes, And. . .

I think that Yes, And. . . brings us back to our magnificence. Isn't it a wonder that we can feel so much? That so much can be simultaneously true?

Yes, And. . .

We humans are such fascinating creatures.

This life is such a fascinating experience.

Yes, and yes and yes yes yes. . . and. . .

143.

What if advice was like prescription medication? Just because it was effective and helpful for one person doesn't mean that it's right for you. In fact, the wrong advice or dose or timing could be very, very damaging to your system.

So, be attentive with what you take into yourself. And be kind if someone else's advice feels like poison to you. And no need to apologize for spitting it out.

Be present to yourself, notice what you need, and move towards that. It takes some practice.

Also: remember that the advice you give, with all the best intentions, may not be right for others. So don't take it personally if it is rejected.

144.

And perhaps, my darling, when you say that you want more time. . . you are really wanting less distraction cluttering up your time. Because if you had additional minutes, or hours, or days and filled them with more of the little distracting bits, well, you haven't gained much, have you?

But if you take the time you have, and reduce the distracting bits – if you amp your calm and focus and clarity – well, then, you arrive precisely at what it is you want. More room to breathe, to move, and more energy.

And so you see, you can get more time by removing clutter and distraction, and by choosing where you place your attention.

Isn't that good to know?

145.

Remember that exquisite self-care means that, sometimes, other people will not get what they want from you.

146.

She (smiling): How are you?
Me (tear-stained): I have a lot of emotions right now.
She: I love that.
We: hug, laugh, cry, laugh, breathe. . .

Feeling very loved, very accepted, very encouraged, very fortunate, and very, very human.

Thank you, friends.

147.

Emotions. . . can be so. . . inconvenient.

148.

And then he smiled and said: "I'm just going to look at you and love you."

And then I smiled and started laughing, because it was not what I expected. And it was exactly what I needed.

149.

We decided to make our own rules. He found a bowling ball. It was blue with swirls and sparkles, and we set it between us on the floor. I sat on a square cushion. He sat directly on the carpet. Our knees did not quite touch. We began to roll the bowling ball in a slow circle, and then brought it gradually to stillness. It looked like a galaxy.

"This is like casting a spell," I said.

"Do you cast many spells?"

"Yes. Don't you?"

And for a moment we simply sat, holding each other with our presence, attention, and soft gaze.

And then I said,

"What's happening on your side?"

And he smiled and said,

"I feel held in a loving embrace."

And I thought: *Yes, you are. This is how it works.*

But I said nothing, choosing silence, and I smiled, and I felt the space between us and around us and, perhaps, within us, glow and flow with a warm connected light.

This is the love and friendship that arises between strangers on a journey, who cross paths, and do not even know each other's names. Sometimes it's just like that.

150.

Finding language for intelligence and all the ways of knowing is a combination of poetry and science – wanting precision and also artful evocation.

I like to remember that "brain" and "mind" are not quite the same thing. And that the body carries its own intelligence and ways of knowing.

And that the brain is only the location of *some* of our neurons – that our nervous system extends far beyond the skull!

Too often the idea of "intelligence" is located within the brain – but it's all so much more than that.

151.

There is a particular pain at being ignored, or forgotten, or when someone simply stops caring – perhaps they got busy, or other things are on their mind, or they've just lost interest in the thread.

Perhaps this is what Puff the Magic Dragon felt. When your friend stops coming to see you, and you don't know why. It takes a while to know they've gone away.

And then you realize the friendship or connection you'd been holding has been dead a long time. They stopped thinking of you with warmth and intention a long time ago.

152.

At first, you seemed to be a Red Rose.

But as I got to know you better, and as you grew and began to open, I began to see how you truly are, and how I had been wrong because there was so much more to you than I realized.

And maybe you always knew it, maybe you were thinking, "Inside I'm the opposite of what you see and think of me."

Or maybe you were unaware of your own magic and it startled you to find it, too, when you did bloom and reveal your innermost self.

Either way, I'm glad you're here and I love you for being just as you are.

Also, you smell really good.

153.

Me: I'm running behind – give me 5 minutes.

He: I'd like to give you the rest of my life.

154.

There are moments so delicious, and when I'm present and completely in them, it fills my whole life. And then a shift, a spark, a curiosity, and I'm off and diving into some new project. I think this is a good way to approach life. Be all in, when you're in the moment, so that you can fill your life to the brim. And then also allow the moment to change, to open to some new delight, and then go do that.

Each moment like that is enough and complete and whole.

And then our appetite and curiosity brings us new moments!

People are afraid that if they are present they will become lazy, or lose their ambition, or fail to accomplish something they have set as a goal.

But the unfolding moment isn't static, my love. To be utterly content by having a good cup of coffee, then walking through Central Park and having a heart-to-heart talk with a friend – this is the sweetness of life, and of enjoying the most simple and fundamental pleasures.

Do not fear this. Allow yourself this pleasure.

You are the only one who can.

155.

Devotion helps when you become lost. (We all become lost, from time to time.)

Devotion is a way to come back again. It is a motive force, it is love, activated.

Devotion has a point of view, and it says *Yes.*

Devotion steps forward or it stands its ground or it circles back.

Devotion is relationship. It is space and it is connection. It is service and humble and powerful.

Devotion is a conscious choosing, and this can steady you on the days you feel tossed by the stormy sea of life.

What do you choose?

Where do you place your attention?

What do you move towards?

Whom do you stand by?

How do you hold this one sweet life?

The answer is the living practice of Devotion.

And if you forget – and, my love, we all do forget from time to time – Devotion is always here for you, waiting with infinite patience and love undiminished.

Devotion has no need for forgiveness. Devotion is allowance and discernment.

156.

Sometimes you feel so Disheartened, and cannot find your way out of that desert. You cannot access the well of Encouragement, you cannot revive your tired heart.

Devotion will help you in those times. Devotion is gentle, and ferocious. Devotion is so steady and willing in its service. Devotion will nudge or carry you, bit by bit. It will breathe life back into your heart.

Devotion can bring you back to life, back to replenishment.

And while you are still caught in waves of pain, or feeling curled up away from the too bright sun and the wind that burns your skin, Devotion will sit beside you in silence and offer its companionship and unflagging belief in your ability to rise again.

Devotion will help you, even to move through tears towards that which awaits on the other side.

157.

You don't need to be in charge of all the things, my love. You don't need to Make Things Happen. You only need to allow Serendipity to find you. You only need to recognize Love when it appears at your door or at your side. You only need to create the circumstances for Magic to happen, and then enjoy its power and delight when it arrives.

158.

This is the part where I would curl up with you and hold you close to me, and feel you breathing, and drink you in. And I would feel you hold me close to you, and we would be entwined, arms and legs, and bodies so close to each other.

I receive and hold all with deep care, tenderness, and reverence.

What a good world it is, and what a good life, as evidenced by the simple fact that we have each other this way.

159.

I can be very needy sometimes. I can be very judgmental, and very self-judging, and also I can be very fearful.

Sometimes I think that I need to pretend that none of these things are true, because I worry that if you knew this about me then you won't like me because you seem to not have those things and I'm afraid of not having my shit together when you seem to have yours together.

I feel like I should know better about all this.

Sometimes this is how it is for me.

And sometimes I have a friend who sees me hiding and calls me out, and says that when I hide it just makes it harder for love to find me.

So I'm wanting to practice not hiding so much, and practice allowing love to find me and be here with me.

And you know, I'm writing this book now about Love. And I'm

remembering another friend who told me, "We write and teach what we most need to learn." So I suppose that's all true also.

Love and Courage to you, all of my lovely and courageous ones.

I am learning.

And thank you for being my friend.

160.

Gently. Keep showing up for yourself. You'll see. And know that ferocious can also be gentle, that powerful can be gentle, that focus and drive and so many things can be approached gently.

Afterword

Most of my writing is never seen by anyone. I show up to the page and write because it feels good to do so.

This is how I know I am a writer. The evidence is undeniable; when I look back I find volumes upon volumes of notebooks filled with words. One page at a time, one word at a time, one gentle pen-stroke at a time, did those pages fill.

How does it all come about?

Gently, my love.

And with deepest and most loving devotion.

And you, too, my love.

You don't need to know what it all adds up to. Just keep showing up. One breath at a time, with deepest and loving devotion, for your own sweet life.

Acknowledgements

Deep thanks to Nestor Perez, for his continued guidance and meditation teachings. Heartfelt gratitude to Dina Amsterdam, for InnerYoga and the gentle, powerful reminder to Be Aware with Care.

Thank you Robin Birdwell for the cover design and encouragement. And a big smile and so much love to my Facebook community, for receiving the earliest draft of this book with such warmth and enthusiasm.

About the Author

Kim Nicol teaches meditation and mindfulness. She has led workshops at the Nasdaq Entrepreneurial Center, law firms, tech start-ups, and global organizations. She lives in San Francisco.

Learn more about her at: kimnicol.com

Made in the USA
Lexington, KY
11 October 2016